Blessed Is The Lord Prayers For The Workplace

STACEY N. COX

STACEY N. COX

Copyright © 2014 Stacey N. Cox

All rights reserved.

ISBN:10: 1-7322781-0-5
ISBN-13: 978-1-7322781-0-3

DEDICATION

This book is dedicated to all those who understand the importance of working and are passionate about closing the gap between their faith and work.

STACEY N. COX

BLESSED IS THE LORD: PRAYER FOR THE WORKPLACE

This book or parts thereof may not be reproduced in any form, stored in a retrieval system, or transmitted in any form by any means—electronic, mechanical, photocopy, recording, or otherwise—without prior written permission of the publisher, except as provided by United States of America Copyright law. Unless otherwise indicated, all Scripture quotations are taken from The Amplified Bible (AMP). The Amplified Bible, Old Testament, Copyright © 1965, 1987 by the Zondervan Corporation. The Amplified New Testament, Copyright © 1954, 1958, 1987 by The Lockman Foundation. Used by permission.

All rights reserved. No part of this publication may be reproduced, distributed, or transmitted in any form or by any means, including photocopying, recording, or other electronic or mechanical methods, without the prior written permission of the author, except in the case of brief quotations embodied in critical reviews and certain other noncommercial uses permitted by copyright law. For permission requests, write to the author at the address below.

Copyright © 2014 Stacey N. Cox

Change of Heart Publishing
11 West Prospect Avenue
Mount Vernon, NY 10550

STACEY N. COX

CONTENTS

Introduction

1. Guidance
2. Your Purpose
3. You and Your Company's Success, Growth & Expansion
4. Difficult Coworkers, Bosses & Customers
5. Problem Resolution in the Workplace
6. God's Favor

STACEY N. COX

INTRODUCTION

After I accepted Christ as my Lord and Savior, many people told me it was not appropriate to discuss religion or talk about God in the workplace. I must admit I was a little confused how cursing and conversations about drinking until short of passing out is appropriate workplace conversation, but God is off limits. I often struggled with this lack of acceptance until I went on a job interview. As I sat in a group interview, the interviewer started referencing scripture to describe the company's expectations. The interviewer had an open Bible on his desk and during the interview was very comfortable talking about the Word of God. In that moment, I heard the Holy Spirit say: "I want you to be comfortable talking about Me in the workplace."

Dealing with others can become a spiritual struggle but with every employer, coworker, manager, customer, project and promotion, God wants *you* to seek Him. *Blessed Is The Lord Prayers for the Workplace* is God's resolution for places of business. Seek God in all matters and He will perfect all things concerning Him. You are His concern. Let's begin!

STACEY N. COX

Guidance

STACEY N. COX

BLESSED IS THE LORD: PRAYER FOR THE WORKPLACE

1

Blessed is the Lord whose love and goodness follow me all the days of my life. Father God, I thank You for opening the door of my current position. I pray for a heart to serve You in my workplace in everything I do. Your grace is sufficient for all that is needed. I come in agreement with Your Word regarding my position, department and place of employment. Bless the gifts and talents of my hand as I prepare for my daily assignment. In all I do, may I work with all of my heart as working for You, Lord and not men.
In Jesus Name, Amen.

Whatever you do [whatever your task may be, work from the soul that is, put in your very best effort], as [something done] for the Lord and not for men. Colossians 3:23 AMP

2

Blessed is the Lord who anoints my head with oil and allows my cup to continuously overflow with His goodness. Into Your hands I commit my work because success, growth and expansion on the job is my portion. Father, You know the plans that You have for me, plans to give me hope and a future. Guide my footsteps as Your Word is a lamp to my feet. Reveal every system, format, operating procedure and relationship formed in secret places that are not of You. I command Your light to shine bright in the dark places. Use

me Lord to bring new business and operation strategies in the workplace that glorify You. Grant me favor in my assignment and put my name before the right people. I come in agreement with Your plans for success on my job.

In Jesus Name, Amen.

Commit your works to the Lord [submit and trust them to Him and your plans will succeed if you respond to His will and guidance.
Proverbs 16:3 AMP

3

Blessed is the Lord whose power is made perfect in my weakness. Father, I stand strong on Your Word even in the middle of negative backlash. Bring healing to those who are hurting and holding on to unforgiveness. I pray that a spirit of forgiveness come upon me so that I may forgive with the level of grace that You have forgiven me. I pray over those who seek to kill, steal and destroy projects, reputations, opportunities and promotions. May healing come to those who are selfish, insecure and manipulative. I choose to stand strong on Your Word and not give up for You will reward my work.

In Jesus Name, Amen.

But as for you, be strong and do not give up, for there is reward for your work. 2 Chronicles 15:7 AMP

4

BLESSED IS THE LORD: PRAYER FOR THE WORKPLACE

Blessed is the Lord who has called me to do a mighty work on my job. Father God use me to set an example for others, to work with integrity and a spirit of excellence, even when management is not looking. Clothe me daily with an enthusiasm to work as if I'm working for You. Anoint me with the wisdom of Solomon for my assignment.
In Jesus Name, Amen.

Not in the way of eye-service working only when someone is watching you and only to please men, but as slaves of Christ, doing the will of God from your heart. Ephesians 6:6 AMP

5

Blessed is the Lord who says, "Let there be light," and there it was. Father let Your light shine in the workplace. Expose every deed done and word spoken that has been hidden in darkness. Your Word is a lamp to my feet. I surrender to You the gifts of my hands. Make me steadfast, immovable and always excelling in the workplace. I know that my work for You is not in vain.
In Jesus Name, Amen.

Therefore, my beloved brothers and sisters, be steadfast, immovable, always excelling in the work of the Lord always doing your best and doing more than is needed], being continually aware that your labor [even to the point of exhaustion in the Lord is not futile nor wasted it is never without purpose.
1 Corinthians 15:58 AMP

Your Purpose

STACEY N. COX

6

Blessed is the Lord who can do all things. No thought or purpose of Yours can be restrained. I can do my assignment through Christ who has strengthened me. Father, I proclaim Your name in this place and may Your power be seen. I surrender the plans of the workplace to You because many are the plans of man, but Your plan and purpose will always prevail. I pray a right alignment with Your Word and the company's vision.
In Jesus Name, Amen.

You shall freely and generously give to him, and your heart shall not be resentful when you give to him, because for this generous thing the Lord your God will bless you in all your work and in all your undertakings.
Deuteronomy 15:10 AMP

7

Blessed is the Lord who has anointed my assignment and made me to be a solution. You have appointed, placed and purposely planted me here as a representative of Christ to bear fruit that will remain long after my assignment is complete. I am strengthened by Your Word to not give up when my assignment seems difficult. May my actions be a reflection of You especially during challenging times.
In Jesus Name, Amen.

And in all things show yourself to be an example of good works with purity in doctrine having the strictest regard for integrity and truth.
Titus 2:7 AMP

8

Blessed is the Lord who gives me the gifts to produce and enjoy the good of my labor. Anoint my hands for this purpose-filled assignment. The workload is heavy, and I can't do it without You. I call on You day and night for guidance to fulfill my workload. Father, I am constantly strengthened and empowered because Your grace is enough. Bless this gift of employment and every relationship, new project and lesson I receive at this company. Give me discernment and wisdom regarding those with whom I labor amongst.

In Jesus Name, Amen.

And also, that every man should eat and drink and see and enjoy the good of all his labor-- it is the gift of God. Ecclesiastes 3:13 AMP

9

Blessed is the Lord whose Word is active, living and full of power. Father bless my coworkers for we are Your fellow workers, and this is Your corporate field. I put every assignment before You as we work together knowing that we're purposed to be here. We will be rewarded according to our own labor, company satisfaction guaranteed.

In Jesus Name, Amen.

BLESSED IS THE LORD: PRAYER FOR THE WORKPLACE

Two are better than one because they have a more satisfying return for their labor. Ecclesiastes 4:9 AMP

10

Blessed is the Lord who is worthy of honor and praise. Father, may I bring Your glory, honor and praise with me on every assignment. May Your fresh breeze enter this building and break strongholds. Your Word is power before my eyes as I enter a territory of favor. You prepared the way for me. You've been with and will continue to be with me in the process.

In Jesus Name, Amen.

I have glorified You down here on the earth by completing the work that you gave Me to do. John 17:4 AMP

STACEY N. COX

You and Your Company's Success, Growth & Expansion

STACEY N. COX

11

Blessed is the Lord who commands fairness. When the enemy comes in like a flood, You will raise up a standard in me. I align myself with the vision of the company and the standard You have set before me. Father, I think on the things of You and work in the spirit of excellence. Thank You for showing me Your wind of favor and loving kindness.

In Jesus Name, Amen.

So, they will fear the name of the Lord from the west and His glory from the rising of the sun. For He will come in like a narrow, rushing stream which the breath of the Lord drives overwhelming the enemy.
Isaiah 59:19 AMP

12

Blessed is the Lord who brings a wind of change. I speak Your Word in this season and trust You with all my heart during this slow season. I rejoice in You in this time of reflection, encouragement, new ideas, improvements and preparation to meet the needs that surpass the expectations of our customers. Bless our labor so it's pleasing in Your sight and meets our customers' needs.

In Jesus Name, Amen.

He must work hard, making an honest living, producing that which is good with his own hands, so that he will have something to share with those in need. Ephesians 4:28 AMP

13

Blessed is the Lord whose goodness and mercy follow me all the days of my life. May Your Word be a great treasure in my heart. You are my shepherd and I shall not want. Father show me how to thoughtfully encourage others to do good work.

In Jesus Name, Amen!

For where your treasure is, there your heart your wishes, your desires; that on which your life centers will be also. Matthew 6:21 AMP

14

Blessed is the Lord who answers the heartfelt and persistent prayers that accomplish much. May my faith take action and see Your effective power at work. Thank You for every victory because the success we are experiencing could only come to pass with the help of the Lord.

In Jesus Name, Amen.

When all our enemies heard about this, all the Gentile nations around us saw it, they lost their confidence; for they recognized that this work had been accomplished with the help of our God.
Nehemiah 6:16 AMP

15

Blessed is the Lord who makes feet like hind's feet and sets me on high places. I enter the high places in union with Christ. I enter the high places with an attitude of gratitude and success. My company is in position to experience victory and success.

In Jesus' Name, Amen!

For you shall eat the fruit of the labor of] your hands, You will be happy and blessed and it will be well with you.
Nehemiah 6:16 AMP

STACEY N. COX

Difficult Coworkers, Bosses & Customers

STACEY N. COX

16

Blessed is the Lord who covers me with His feathers; under Your wings, I take refuge. Your faithfulness is my shield and rampart. I speak Your Word over my life. I am strong and courageous and will not tremble or become fearful of my job. Difficulty has come but I know that You have prepared the way for me. I trust You, Lord for You will never fail me or abandon me.

In Jesus Name, Amen.

Be strong and courageous, do not be afraid or tremble in dread before them, for it is the Lord your God who goes with you. He will not fail you or abandon you. Deuteronomy 31:6 AMP

17

Blessed is the Lord, my God for You are with me and I will not fear. You have strengthened me, and I am assured that You will help in these times. I trust You and confidently rely on You with all of my heart. I acknowledge and recognize You in these times. You are removing obstacles so that my company's path is smooth and straight.

In Jesus Name, Amen!

Trust in and rely confidently on the Lord with all your heart and do not rely on your own insight or understanding. In all your ways know

and acknowledge and recognize Him, and He will make your paths straight and smooth removing obstacles that block your way.
Proverbs 3:5-6 AMP

18

Blessed is the Lord who upholds and sustains the righteous who seek Him. Lord, You know the days of the blameless and all our inheritance will continue forever. Father, help Your chosen one to have a compassionate heart with kindness, humility, meekness and patience, bearing with others while learning to forgive anyone for any grievance committed. As You have forgiven me, may I forgive others. In Jesus Name, Amen!

Hatred stirs up strife, but love covers and overwhelms all transgressions forgiving and overlooking another's faults. Proverbs 10:12 AMP

19

Blessed is the Lord of Light and the great I am. Father, You sent the Holy Spirit to be a helper, comforter, advocate, intercessor, counselor and strengthener to stand in Your place, represent You and act on Your behalf to teach all things. Peace is my portion. The perfect peace that You have given is calming in every circumstance, giving me

BLESSED IS THE LORD: PRAYER FOR THE WORKPLACE

courage and strength in every challenge.

In Jesus Name, Amen!

Do not participate in the worthless ana unproductive deeds of darkness, but instead expose them by exemplifying personal integrity, moral courage, and godly character. Ephesians 5:11

20

Blessed is the Lord whose power is perfected and completed, showing most effective in my weakness. As iron sharpens iron, I pray that my submission to You is evident in the workplace and causes me to be an influence on others through discussions. Your loving kindness and mercy are more than enough and always available to me regardless of situations and circumstances. I am strengthened in You despite insults, hindrances, distractions and conversations that may seem discouraging in the workplace. Father, You are strong when I am weak. Show Yourself mighty and strong today. I continually pray over those who don't know You and those who do not understand Your Word. I pray peace over this office, our customers, management and all business affairs. Saturate my heart with joy and help me to live peaceably with others.

In Jesus Name, Amen.

Be unceasing and persistent in prayer.
1 Thessalonians 5:17 AMP

Problem Resolution in the Workplace

STACEY N. COX

BLESSED IS THE LORD: PRAYER FOR THE WORKPLACE

21

Blessed is the Lord who trains my hands for war and gives my fingers skills for battle. Guide my words Lord as I speak to others because soft, gentle, and thoughtful answers turn away wrath, but harsh, painful and careless words stir up anger. May I think on the things that are right, gracious and proper in the sight of all of my coworkers and customers. I give every problematic situation to You. You said to never avenge myself but to leave the way open for Your judicial righteousness. Vengeance is Yours so I take my hands and my mouth off of the situation. I pray over those who seek to bring harm, hurt or danger. Those that follow You will not be overcome by evil but will overcome by doing good. I thank You, Father for being in the details and causing peace in my workplace.
In Jesus Name, Amen!

A soft and gentle and thoughtful answer turns away wrath, but harsh and painful and careless words stir up anger. Proverbs 15:1 AMP

22

Blessed is the Lord of peacemakers and peace maintainers. I pray over those who express the character of You, Lord. We are blessed and spiritually calm with life, joy and Your

favor upon us. We shall not take revenge nor bear any grudge against anyone. We will love our neighbors, acquaintances, associates, companions and those in authority as we love ourselves.
In Jesus Name, Amen!

You shall not take revenge nor bear any grudge against the sons of your people, but you shall love your neighbor acquaintance, associate, companion as yourself; I am the Lord.
Leviticus 19:18 AMP

23

Blessed is the Lord who is faithful and just to forgive me of my sins and cleanse me from unrighteousness. Father, forgive me for every word I have spoken and acted upon that did not reflect You. May I forgive with the grace with which You have forgiven me. I submit myself to You and allow You to work out this situation so that dignity and self-respect are maintained in my life.
In Jesus Name, Amen!

But I say to you, do not resist an evil person who insults you or violates your rights but whoever slaps you on the right cheek, turn the other toward him also simply ignore insignificant insults or trivial losses and do not bother to retaliate—maintain your dignity, your self-respect, your poise. Matthew 5:39, AMP

24

Blessed is the Lord who raised a standard of behavior from me. Help me Father to be quick to hear, being a careful and thoughtful listener of words said and not said. May I speak words of truth that encourage others. Help me to be patient, reflective and forgiving of the resentful, deep-seated anger of others. I pray that the atmosphere and culture of this corporation will stand on the righteousness of God. In Jesus Name, Amen!

So, get rid of all uncleanness and all that remains of wickedness, and with a humble spirit receive the word of God which is implanted actually rooted in your heart, which is able to save your souls.
James 1:21, AMP

25

Blessed is the Lord whose blessings bring well-being, happiness and protection. Father, as employees of this company, I pray that we would be like-minded, sympathetic, kind-hearted, courteous and compassionate towards one another. Lord, please provide protection, well-being and contentment for my coworkers. I pray that we would learn to enjoy life and see good in our days. May we avoid thinking evil towards or about one another. Keep our tongues free from evil and our lives free from speaking treachery and deceit.

In Jesus Name, Amen.

The one who wants to enjoy life and see good days good—whether apparent or not, must keep his tongue free from evil and his lips from speaking guile treachery, deceit. 1 Peter 3:8-11 AMP

God's Favor

BLESSED IS THE LORD: PRAYER FOR THE WORKPLACE

26

Blessed is the Lord who loads us daily with grace and blessings. I submit myself to You as a living sacrifice, holy and acceptable. I pray favor with management, co-workers, vendors and customers. I seek your strength and wisdom to honor the requests and demands of the company. May we be on one accord to build, enhance, grow and expand the position of this company in the marketplace.
In Jesus Name, Amen.

I have found favor in the sight of the king, and if it pleases the king to grant my petition and to do as I request, may the king and Haman come to the banquet that I will prepare for them; and tomorrow I will do as the king says and express my request. Esther 5:8 AMP

27

Blessed is the Lord whose favor makes a way for me. Father, Your love gives me strength and Your favor opens doors.
In Jesus Name, Amen!

But God clearly shows and proves His own love for us, by the fact that while we were still sinners, Christ died for us. Romans 5:8 AMP

28

Blessed is the Lord whose favor is for a lifetime. I give You an early morning shout of joy. Your favor and grace made me stand strong like a mountain. I rejoice in You.
In Jesus Name, Amen!

His anger is but for a moment, and his favor is for a lifetime. Weeping may tarry for the night, but joy comes with the morning.
Psalm 30:5 AMP

29

Blessed is the Lord who strengthens and encourages me. Father, You hold me up when I start to grow weary or become discouraged in doing good. You have fed, guided, shielded and restored me. Your name brings me protection and strength. I reap a harvest of Your favor.
In Jesus Name, Amen!

Let us not grow weary or become discouraged in doing good, for at the proper time we will reap, if we do not give in. Galatians 6:9 AMP

30

Blessed is the Lord who surrounds me with favor. Confidence in You brings a multitude of favor in my life. I walk in an abundance of favor. Favor is my portion.
In Jesus Name, Amen!

Do not, therefore, fling away your fearless] confidence, for it has a glorious and great reward. Hebrews 10:35 AMP

STACEY N. COX

Forgiveness

31

Blessed is the Lord who is my rock and my fortress. You lead and guide me for Your name's sake. Lead me in truth and teach me Your ways. Father, forgive me for every word I spoke out of alignment with Your Word. Forgive me for holding resentment in my heart towards others. Forgive me for holding bitterness and unforgiveness in my heart. Forgive me for every unkind word spoken out of anger. I have the peace, righteousness, security and triumph over opposition. Thank You for showing me the hearts of the people with which I labor and how to effectively intercede while working. Your favor flows through me like a river.

A cool breeze of favor has entered the office. A fresh wind of favor restores and maintains the corporate vision and mission. Father, Your blessings of favor has brought corporate advancement, financial security, fulfilling purpose, success and stability.
In Jesus Name, Amen!

In that day, You will not [need to] ask Me about anything. I assure you and most solemnly say to you, whatever you ask the Father in My name as My representative, He will give you. John 16:23, AMP

STACEY N. COX

OTHER BOOKS BY STACEY

Blessed Is The Lord: Prayers For My Daily Walk
A book of prayers to open the door of your life to God.

Walking In Your Purpose

A book of devotionals to you hear God's plan and wisdom for living on purpose.

Follow the Author on Social Media

Facebook Gatekeeper's Marketplace Prayer

Twitter @prays4themarketplace

Youtube Gatekeeper's Marketplace Prayer

www.ingramcontent.com/pod-product-compliance
Lightning Source LLC
Chambersburg PA
CBHW061301040426
42444CB00010B/2460